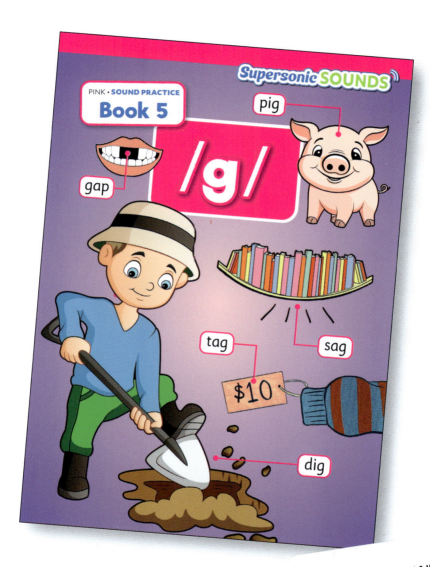

Minneapolis, Minnesota

Teaching Tips

This book focuses on the phoneme **/g/**.

Getting Started

- Review the focus phoneme of the book with readers.
- Model the sound and have readers practice themselves.

Using the Book

- Ask readers to read the words on the pages with the colorful borders, using the focus sound as their guide.
- Turn the page and check the illustration next to the word to confirm accuracy.
- As you read new words, review the word bank on the left-hand pages of the book.

Reviewing

- Encourage readers to independently reread all of the words on pages 22–23.
- Have them complete the activity on page 24 for continued practice with the focus phoneme.
- Extend the learning by asking readers if they know any other words containing the focus phoneme.

For more information, write to Bearport Publishing, 5357 Penn Avenue South, Minneapolis, MN 55419.

sag

sag

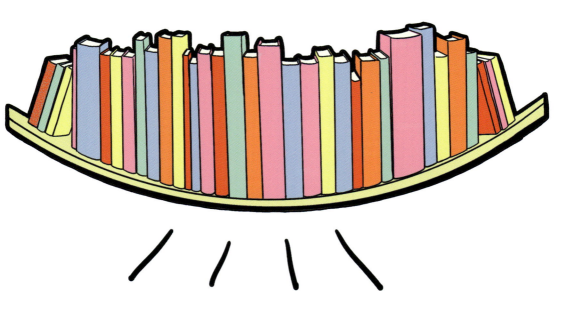

sag

tag

tag

tag

sag

tag

gap

gap

gap

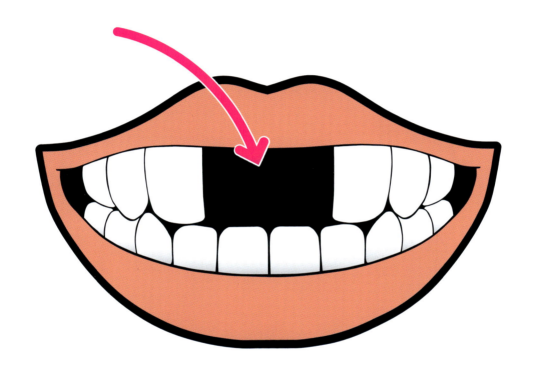

sag

tag

gap

pig

pig

pig

17

sag

tag

gap

pig

dig

dig

dig

sag

tag

gap

dig

pig

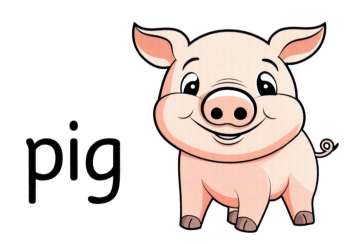

Say the sound and trace the letter with your finger.

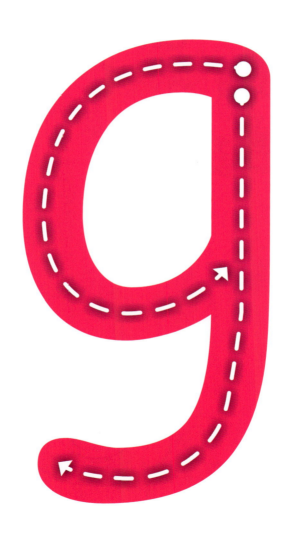